# SHEKHINAH SPEAKS

# SHEKHINAH SPEAKS

## JOY LADIN

*Best,*
*Joy Ladin*

selva oscura press • chicago, illinois

Published by selva oscura press
selvaoscurapress.com

First Edition

ISBN 979-8-9856636-0-0

Design and typesetting by Margaret Tedesco
Text set in Trajan Pro and Adobe Caslon Pro
Printing: McNaughton & Gunn

Cover art: *The Prophet II*, David Orr, ©2007. Courtesy of the artist.

Distributed by Small Press Distribution
1341 Seventh Street, Berkeley, CA 94710
www.spdbooks.org

a 501(c)(3) nonprofit

# TABLE OF CONTENTS

# A Note on the Poems

*Shekhinah Speaks* is an effort to give voice to the Shekhinah, described in mystical Jewish tradition as the immanent, feminine aspect of God who dwells with human beings and shares our lives, joys, and sorrows. What we feel, she feels; what we endure, she endures.

Tradition imagines the Shekhinah as a passive, mostly silent presence. These poems tune in to a Shekhinah who never stops talking to you who, to her, is each and all of us.

The Shekhinah's words aren't mine. The language of each poem is sampled from two source texts, one drawn from the Book of Isaiah and the other from *Cosmopolitan*, whose content or imagery resonate with one another. The one exception is "Comfort Animal," written before I adopted this approach, only some of which is drawn from the source texts.

The twenty-two poems (one for each letter of the Hebrew alphabet) are presented in sequence, as human conventions require. But to the Shekhinah, who exists outside time and space, they are all being spoken to each of us simultaneously, at every moment of our lives, which, from her perspective, happen continuously, and forever.

She is sometimes called daughter and sometimes sister
and sometimes mother. She is all
and everything is in her.

—Zohar 2:100b

# Fetus in Distress

For a long time I've kept silent,
been quiet and held myself back.
But now, like a woman in childbirth,
I cry out, I gasp and pant.

—Isaiah 42:14

"Why Are American Women Dying in Childbirth?" *Cosmopolitan*. December 12, 2015.


I cry out, I gasp and pant,
unfail your organs, open your eyes,
irritate your nervous system

by straightening your crooked places,
giving you hands and hallways,
hours, mountains, backwoods frying pans.

Freedom flows from me into you,
rivulets of justice, delight
and terror, love and wilderness.

You don't know,
you can't understand.
You keep crying out,

drip-drip-dragging
your soul like an IV behind you
on your way to the sea

or the weekend, or to prison, or bed,
begging to be born
into some other kind of body,

begging not to be born at all,
to be held forever
like breath.

You don't know, you can't understand:
clots or sepsis, hemorrhage
or cardiac arrest,

I feel what you feel,
bear what you bear,
lingering among your acids,

tearing myself to shreds,
transfusing your suffering
with my glory,

*you are* with *I am.*

# I.

# REVELATION

## STILL BORN

> See, the Lord rides on a swift cloud . . .
>
> —Isaiah 19:1

> "19-year-old Skylar Richardson Says She Had a Stillborn Baby.
> So Why Is She on Trial for Murder?" *Cosmopolitan*. March 14, 2018.

You're still being born,
still trying to understand
what you are

and where I am,
inside or outside, attached
or disattached;

still digging, still scraping,
still filling with time,
still buried, still growing,

still waiting to be delivered.
I know. I'm the neighbor
who's always watching; the teacher

who's sometimes kind; the mother
who sees how hungry you are;
the doctor who makes you sick.

Sometimes I stagger you with terror
but I also cover
your body with flowers, pinks and sweetheart roses;

when they wilt, I remain,
before you're born,
and there in the casket,

you still are my favorite color, a cloud
I continue to ride
even when you're no longer moving, a love

into which I keep falling
even when you're no one, nothing,
stillborn or miscarried,

I still surround you
like a uterus, and you
are still my baby.

# MELTING AWAY

> "... you say to yourself,
> 'I am, and there is no one besides me.'"
>
> —Isaiah 47:10
>
> "The Scary, Scary Way Your Friends Are Losing Weight."
> *Cosmopolitan.* February 12, 2019.

I sit in the stubble of your heart,
listening to you say *I am*.
I am, you say,

and there is no one besides me,
by which you mean
no one to remember, no one to love

your wise and childish,
tender, obsessive, intermittent selves
melting together, melting away.

*I am*, I say, but you don't hear me.
On good days,
you wish I were there.

On better days, you crave me.
On the best days, you feel me
sitting amidst the brokenness of your body,

your strange shiny pleasures
and cardiac butterflies,
lifting the veil of your darkness,

setting your dust on fire.
*I am*, I say,
*and there is no one besides me*,

and for a moment you know
it's you I'm calling,
that I am the love

into which you're falling,
evaporating,
one *I am* at a time,

the part of you—
the only part—
that isn't melting away.

# Forgetting

Can a woman forget her baby,
or disown the child of her womb?
Though she might forget,
I could never forget you.

—Isaiah 49:14–15

"What It's Like to Lose Your Entire Memory." *Cosmopolitan*. December 12, 2015.

You don't remember anything.
How I formed you in your mother's womb;
nursed you; bathed you; taught you to talk;

led you to springs of water.
I sang your name before you were born;
I'm singing your name now.

You're clueless as an infant.
When I tell you to shout for joy,
you hear a bicycle, or a cat.

Sometimes, memories of me come back
like children you forgot you had:
a garden; a bride; an image of your mother,

a best friend, a brother, or a cop, or snow, or afternoon.
Whose are these, you wonder.
Then you forget, and feel forgotten,

like an infant
who falls asleep at the breast
and wakes up hungry again.

Your mother might forget you, child,
but I never forget.
Your name is engraved

on the palms of my hands.
I shower you
with examples of my love—

bees and birds,
librarians, life skills,
emotions, sunlight, compassion.

Nothing connects.
Every dawn, every generation,
I have to teach you again.

This is water;
this is darkness;
this is a body

fitting your description.
That's a crush.
This is an allergic reaction.

This is your anger.
This is mine.
This is me

reminding you to eat;
turn off the stove;
take your medication.

This is the realization
that I am yours
and you are mine. This is you

forgetting.

# FRAGMENTATION

When you walk through the fire,
you will not be burned;
the flames will not set you ablaze.

—Isaiah 43:2

"I Have 13 Different Identities Living Inside of Me. Here's What Our Lives Are Like."
*Cosmopolitan*. October 29, 2018.

Who holds your pieces together,
pieces that can't see, pieces that can't hear, pieces
blotted out by terror?

You don't remember.
You have so many histories
and only one body, one name

and so many identities
living and loving inside you
the way you live and love

in me, no more or less real
than anyone else,
no less splintered,

no closer to understanding
why I summon you by name.
You don't know what I'm talking about.

You don't even know I'm talking.
I'm a deep dive
you don't remember taking

into your terror
that you can't do anything
or that you can,

but only by being a different person,
different from yourself,
different from me.

Don't be afraid.
I'm the fire through which you're walking,
protecting the pieces

you're afraid of losing
or maybe just afraid of,
the children who suffer

and never grow older,
the children who were never born
and the children who are nothing

but gaps in your memory.
How many are there?
It doesn't matter.

I cup every other
into which you're broken,
the jackals, the owls,

the self-harming darkness,
the splinters of shame and despair
that tell you you deserve

all the hate you get.
I hold them, so you can let them go.
I remember, so you can forget.

I'm making you into something new.
Something unafraid.
Something infinite.

I'm the labyrinth
you feel lost inside. The ghost
who never ghosts you,

whose haunting keeps you alive.

## REAL TRUE GHOST STORY

> I have put my words in your mouth
> and covered you
> with the shadow of my hand . . .
>
> —Isaiah 51:6
>
> "10 Terrifying Real Ghost Stories to Tell at Your Next Girls' Night."
> *Cosmopolitan.* October 16, 2018.


Something is there, you think,
something that holds you
from birth to death

like an antelope caught in a net
as heavens go up in smoke
and worlds wear out like garments.

Something that staggers you,
dries up your waters,
drains you to the dregs

by whispering *I am*.
You aren't paralyzed
but can't get away,

can't apologize, can't hide, can't pretend
the way you did when you were a kid
that you've already died.

Something is there that never sleeps.
Something that can't be crushed or killed
shoves its words into your mouth,

forcing doors you try to close
by whispering *I am*.
You wonder if any of this actually happens

but you never wonder
why you feel so sick
when *I am* masses

in your mouth, in your bed,
in the unexplained noise of forever
moving furniture

in your head. On the other side
of whatever you are,
there's nothing but *I am*,

a whisper that stumbles
out of the kitchen
and crawls across your skin:

time; a bowl;
a drink of water; a nightmare
trying to wake you up

by singing in your ear.

# AWAKE

Awake, awake . . .
clothe yourself with strength!

—Isaiah 52

"What Really Happens When You're in a Coma." *Cosmopolitan*. February 5, 2019.



You dream I'm looking down on you
like a light on a ceiling
as though you are a thing

and I am a thing,
a light you aren't,
shining down

on a body
you can't escape
even in dreams, like this one

in which you dream
you're awake, trying to awake
to the light that holds you together

like sticky surgical tape
even when you're a vibrating ruin, a mistake
that keeps making mistakes,

too hurt,
too convinced you're nothing
to understand or explain

the light you dream you see,
sassy, dancing,
clothing you in splendor,

glorying in your glory.
That's when you're awake.

# REVELATION

"I revealed myself to those who didn't ask for me"

—Isaiah 65:1

"I Posed in a Bikini in Times Square." Cosmopolitan. July 13, 2018.

You whisper, grin, push me away, question
whether I'm really there, tell yourself
it doesn't matter

even if I am. Sometimes
you provoke me to my face.
Usually, though, you keep yourself busy,

eating food that makes you hungry,
worrying about money
and what to do with your body,

eager to pay attention
to anything
but who you are to me. You

are a vigil I keep;
a flock I pasture;
a grape on the vine

still bursting with blessing
even at the end of harvest,
and I'm the light

you're afraid of losing,
the light revealing
what it means to be human.

Not an indecipherable mess; not a pot
of meat and feeling,
or a headstone covered in body paint,

or a burning garden, or irony sweating.
A new song
you and I are singing,

me through you and you through me,
about the earth and heaven
and the love

you and I are making.

# II.

# READY

# COME LET US REASON TOGETHER

> Come, let us reason together:
> though your sins are scarlet,
> they shall be white as snow.
>
> —Isaiah 1:18
>
> "The Duggar Parents Aren't Victims. They Are Perpetrators."
> *Cosmopolitan.* June 4, 2015.

Your head is sick; your heart is sick. Bruised
from your sole to your crown,
you hide your devastation under your clothes

even though I'm right here,
replacing the poisons in your blood
with my oxygen.

I know what you've done, and haven't,
where you like to be touched
and why you think you should be punished,

but don't confuse me with conceptions of God
that sneak between your body and soul
and shame what I delight in.

I'm not a conception of God.
I'm a burning city, a moon full of blood,
a wound to be washed, soothed, protected.

You think I come to you for sex?
You're an angel I make in the snow;
a prayer I offer; a trauma I bear

because you can't live without me
and I want you to live.
Sometimes you see me in the mirror,

sometimes in your bed,
sometimes I'm a thread
you follow back to the pleasure

I take in the body, your body, I made
to be a festival and a feast,
a booth in a cucumber field

outside the structures of oppression
that hold you, rear you, put you to sleep,
rape you through your clothes.

Come, let us reason together.
Stop doing evil; start doing good;
learn to tell one from the other.

You are born to burn for justice
as a garden burns for water.
That's why I come, night after night:

so you and I
can burn for justice
together.

# SHAME

Woe to the one who says to a father,
  "What have you begotten?"
or to a mother,
  "What have you brought to birth?"

—Isaiah 45:10

"I Had an Abortion in Alabama, and My Neighbors Shamed Me."
*Cosmopolitan.* May 28, 2019

Ashamed of what you are and aren't,
you struggle to stay connected,
part of the family, part of the culture

that sometimes makes you feel like a monster,
telling yourself
you're the opposite of brave,

that whatever you are is the opposite
of what I meant to make.
How dare you question

what I create?
Your shame and your panic,
your sex and your rage,

where you're broken
and where you break—
I bore them, I bear them, I open the gates

of privilege and stigma
so even you can see
the image—my image—

in which you are made.
You can hide from everyone, child,
but you can't hide from me.

I'm your calamity and your queen,
the truth from which there's no protection,
the heaven that stretches equally

over victory and shame.
I foretold you long ago. Declared
to the ends of the earth

I would be your potter
and you would be my clay.
A storehouse I'd fill with treasure.

A habitation for my name.
Matter fashioned into revelation.
A cloud

from which I rain.

# RECONSTRUCTION

> Who is he is trying to teach? . . .
> Children weaned from their milk?
> Those just taken from the breast?
>
> —Isaiah 28:9

> "These Cancer Patients Wanted to Get Rid of Their Breasts for Good.
> Their Doctors Had Other Ideas." *Cosmopolitan.* September 6, 2018.

You're lucky to be alive
but you don't feel lucky.
You feel like a world on fire.

You want to opt out,
to be flat, a pocket
of wishful skin

instead of a covenant with death.
Instead of remembering
how you've been violated,

a little here, a little there,
morning by morning,
snare by snare,

you wish you could move freely—
run and swim,
stretch out on a bed,

reshape the body
that feels like layers of clothes
concealing a tongue of stretched-out dough

and make it a place
you don't have to hide,
a place where glory

overflows your scars.
What if you knew
I've torn apart

your signed and witnessed
covenant with death,
restoring your range of motion,

giving you refuge,
giving you rest?
Little by little, you'll hear my voice.

Little by little, you'll know
that you are my diadem,
my hailstorm of laughter,

milk from the breast
of my righteousness.
Instead of the body

you never wanted,
you'll see land you can plant, and water,
nuance, sexuality, summer.

Instead of scars,
grain turning into bread.
Where you hoped, at most, to see nothing,

justice ripening like a fig
you're ready to swallow
as soon as it fills your hand.

# FAST

"Is this the fast I require of you?"

—Isaiah 58:5

"Nine Things a Nutritionist Wants You to Know About Fasting"
*Cosmopolitan*. September 8, 2017.

I hunger for you
to hunger for me,
but instead, you feed upon and feed

food chains of oppression,
forsakenness, and need
you train yourself not to see,

ignoring, reducing,
eliminating entirely
the reality of me,

of my hunger for you
to hunger for justice as you hunger
for calories and sleep,

my hunger for you to feast
by metabolizing your days and weeks
into food you share

and springs of water,
answering cries for help
and making Earth a garden again

by letting my glory
dawn through your pain, *I am*
through your flesh.

## THE G-SPOT

To the eunuchs . . . who choose what pleases me . . .
I will give within my temple and its walls
a memorial and a name . . .

—Isaiah 56:4

"The G-Spot Doesn't Exist." *Cosmopolitan*. April 13, 2020.

You're tired of trying,
of having to try,
tired of feeling like a border line,

an unasked-for sacrifice,
of sticking the fingers
of your soul inside

to find
some spot, some center,
in which you're sure

I'm taking pleasure
even when you don't care
about justice or injustice,

salvation or righteousness;
even when you feel like nothing,
not a world or a mystery

or a dog that can't bark
or a dream I don't remember,
you know it must be there,

farther down, or all around,
in forests or mountains,
nerves or appetites,

the love I made you
to discover,
the part of you that feels—

that knows—
you're a Sabbath I keep,
a prayer I answer; that your longing

is my longing,
your rapture, my rapture; that you
are my here-and-now

and I am your forever.

# LIKENESS

> . . . the Lord, who is hiding his face . . .
>
> —Isaiah 8:17
>
> "The Amish Keep to Themselves. And They're Hiding a Horrifying Secret."
> *Cosmopolitan.* January 14, 2020

Like me, you're hidden
in skin, in time,
pinned like me

to a world you endure,
in which you hover,
holy and ordinary,

full of blood and suffering,
rejected, forgotten,
shoved to one side,

mouthed and named
in the language of shame
instead of your mother tongue—

my tongue,
the language of revelation.
Like me, you can't escape

the world that's inside you,
waiting to be healed, to be forgiven,
waiting for you

to be less like a victim,
less like a crime,
less like a body grabbed at dusk, less

like saying nothing
and more like the face
you think I'm hiding.

More like woods,
and wings, and water.
More like conceiving, and giving birth.

More like overflowing.

# READY

Fear not, I am the one who helps you . . .

—Isaiah 41:13

"7 Empowering Life Lessons from 'Buffy the Vampire Slayer.'"
*Cosmopolitan*. March 10, 2017

Are you ready to be strong?

Are you ready to follow me beyond
the fear that warns you
to hold your tongue

when cruelty and hopelessness,
degradation and evil,
stab you through the heart?

Fear likes you this way,
self-loathing and numb,
believing you're no one

I'd ever choose,
a worm in a tunnel,  dust in a gale,
a nameless pool of blood

I could never love.
I summon them all to judgment,
the fears that stalk you

to the ends of the earth,
the shame and disgrace
that nail you in your place,

everything that gets in the way
of you responding when I say
"Don't be afraid."

Don't be afraid.
I was here before fear
and I'm there beyond it,

opening fountains,
trampling kings underfoot,
calling you to me

across generations
by paths you haven't walked,
by ways you cannot imagine.

I'm the mother who really sees,
the father who understands
you, every version,

real and imagined, future and past,
cypress and desert, queer fluid light,
thresher of mountains, solitary pine.

You have nothing to fear
and nothing to prove.
Are you ready

to be strong? Time
to remake the world.

# III.

## I Do

# SINGING

Sing out O barren one, who has not given birth,
break out into song, shout for joy,
one who had no labor pains . . .

—Isaiah 54:1

"Why This Woman Is Proud to Be Known as 'The Pageant Queen Without a Uterus.'"
*Cosmopolitan.* January 20, 2015.


Before you were a fetus,
before you were an egg,
you were a song

I was already singing,
a promise
I'd already kept.

I stretch out your curtains,
strengthen your pegs,
make room inside you for the world

I created you to share. You
are my embryo
and I am your womb;

you're my labor pains
and I'm the mother pushing you
to cry, to talk, to stand for something,

to stop being scared
of the joy
rising like waters in the days of Noah,

flooding your foundations,
crowning your head,
answering every question

I created you to ask.
Why you feel incomplete,
like a tiara without a pageant.

Why you mistake affliction for love
and love, my love,
for affliction.

Why you just start crying
when, for a moment, you hear me sing
the secret you forget you're keeping: you

are the child of a queen.
Why it always feels like the first time to you,
the first shaking of your mountains,

the first bursting into flame,
the very first season
of your first reality show

on which a queen with a whirlwind
where a uterus should be
whose presence fills you with fear

keeps waiting for you
to say "I do"
to the love, my love,

that never stops singing
and follows you
everywhere.

# SPLENDOR

> Go into the rocks, hide in the ground
>     from the fearful presence . . .
>
> —Isaiah 2:10

> "Psychologists Explain Why Micro-Cheating Is the Latest Infidelity Trend Everyone
> Is Talking About." *Cosmopolitan*. January 21, 2018.

Of course you're full of fear.

The closer I come
the more you feel
like a cave, or a rock,

or a hole in the ground.
You don't know how to relate
to splendor

that has no form, no face, no sweetness
you know how to taste, no love
you know how to feel.

Of course you want to flee.
I make you feel little,
make you feel mean,

like something that needs to be removed,
beaten into another form,
thrown altogether away.

You long to feel treasured
and embraced
by someone who has fingers and a face,

someone like you
who's full of holes,
who knows what it means

to strain,
to wait. Someone
who isn't always there,

a terror you can't shake,
a bond you cannot sever,
a light you've longed for

and tried to flee
since it first tempted you
from rocks and caves

and holes in the ground
into the splendor
of humanity.

## Your Body

Heaven is my throne, and the earth is my footstool.
Where is the house you will build for me?
Where will my resting place be?"

—Isaiah 66:1

"Inside the Scam of the 'Purity' Movement." *Cosmopolitan.* February 5, 2019.


You keep trying to escape
the body I love,
the blazing crush

of physicality, impurity, and shame
separating you from yourself,
from your soul, from me,

the body I formed
in your mother's womb,
delivered, dandled, nursed and comforted,

the body that fails you
in so many ways,
through which you struggle to materialize

the way tomorrow struggles
to materialize through today;
blessing through pain; love

through the flesh I made
to be a place
where you and I can rest,

hang out, go crazy for one another,
marry, say goodbye, apologize,
consume and burn like incense,

can plead, pledge, proclaim,
be held and protected, given and accepted,
born, and born again.

It's me you feel
moving inside you, my presence
that's so hard to reconcile

with your sexual nature
and the nature of sex
that sometimes you feel violated,

devoured,
tell yourself that you're no good,
imagine me

demanding you preach
gospels of fire, gospels of bone, gospels
of coming to an end.

I didn't make you to end.
I made you a whirlwind
of appetites and offerings

I never stop wanting,
ceremony and sacrifice,
wine and reckoning,

comedy, coolness, birthing and healing,
falling in love,
romance, yes, and sex.

Your body is a stream from which I drink,
a hand I hold,
a nipple I lick,

a story I tell over and over,
a Sabbath I keep for pleasure;
a way of being alone;

a way of being together;
my choir, my throne,
my crazy music,

my dog-eared paperback.

# BODY PAINTING

He shapes it in a human form,
the human form in all its glory . . .

—Isaiah 44:13

"What It Was Like Painting a Nearly Naked Ariana Grande for Her
'God Is A Woman' Music Video." *Cosmopolitan*. July 19, 2018.


I dance and sing, pool and flower,
folding you into human form,
showing you how to breathe.

It's always your first time
and your last
being painted with a body,

brushed with skin,
with shape,
with brevity and beauty.

I know it's hard to be human,
to be my medium,
my canvas and my muse,

a nearly naked image of God
that can't stop bleeding
and revealing

the spirit that paints you
with hair and time and nerves,
sings you, dances you,

makes you what you are.
Like grass in a meadow
existence springs up

when you pay attention,
colorized, ticklish, just like you,
waiting to be witnessed,

waiting to be loved.
Me too.
I know it's hard to see and feel,

inspire and embrace
the process of your own creation,
the coals and hammers,

glories and terrors,
that cast you into human form
and mark you with my image.

I'm forest when you flower;
water when you thirst;
bread when you're hungry;

real as a hammer,
I rebuild your ruins,
rain on your dry earth,

dance and sing
your purples and your blues
at the center of the universe

I create through you.

# Comfort Animal

Comfort, comfort my people . . .

—Isaiah 40:1

"Here's Absolutely Everything You Need to Know About Getting an Emotional Support Animal." *Cosmopolitan*. February 9, 2018.

A voice says, "Your punishment has ended."
You never listen to that voice. You really suck
at being comforted.

Another voice says, "Cry."
That voice *always* gets your attention,
keeps you thinking

about withered flowers and withering grass
and all the ways you're like them.
Hard to argue with that.

Death tramples you, an un-housebroken pet
trailing prints and broken stems,
pooping anxiety, PTSD, depression.

It's better to be animal than vegetable
but best of all is to be spirit
flying first or maybe business class

with your emotional support animal, your body,
curled in your lap,
soaring with you

above the sense of loss you've mistaken
for the closest to God you can get.
You want to cry about something? Cry about that.

Who do you think created
the animals to which you turn for comfort,
dogs, miniature horses, monkeys, ferrets,

hungers you know how to feed,
fears you know how to quiet?
I form them, fur them,

it's my warmth radiating from their bodies,
my love that answers
the love you lavish upon them.

Your deserts and desolations are highways I travel,
smoothing your broken places,
arranging stars and constellations

to light your wilderness.
Sometimes I play the shepherd;
sometimes I play the lamb;

sometimes I appear as death,
which makes it hard to remember
that I'm the one who assembles your atoms,

crowns your dust with consciousness.
I take you everywhere,
which is why, wherever you go,

I'm there,
keeping you hydrated, stroking your hair,
laughing when you chase your tail,

gathering you in
more tenderly than any mother.
I'm the reason

your valleys are being lifted up,
the source of your life laid bare.
Mine is the voice that decrees—

that begs—
your anguish to end.
When you suffer, I suffer.

Comfort me
by being comforted.

# GETTING REAL

Why do you say, . . .
"My way is hidden from the LORD,
my cause is disregarded . . ."?

—Isaiah 40:27

"8 Reasons to Stop Looking for 'The One.'" *Cosmopolitan*. April 6, 2018

Get real, you say.

You don't know how
to comfort me, to lift me up,
to be a being

who withers and falls
and still reveals my glory.
You feel lost when you can't find me

and lost when I'm there,
like a drop in a bucket,
dust on a scale, not real enough

and much too real.
You don't know why I'm here
flowering among your fear

of being judged, uprooted, pointless,
a fleeting feeling of irritation,
a complaint I can't share

because I'm the one
who judges, uproots,
and whirls your dust away.

I am. I do. Like a grasshopper
trying to number
stars it cannot see, it's hard for you to imagine

and harder to believe
I choose you every day;
give you life, and soul, and strength;

that before Earth was founded, I already knew
my love would flower
in your wilderness, my glory

in your face.

# I Do

Unhappy, storm-tossed, uncomforted one!

—Isaiah 54:11

"12 Achingly Beautiful Bridal Trends You'll Want to Steal for Your Wedding."
*Cosmopolitan*. October 12, 2016.

Unhappy, storm-tossed, uncomforted one,
you ache for me
even though I'm here,

stitching kindness and desolation,
flowering and fear,
into walls and gates and battlements

from which you can always see
that you don't have to ache for me—
I'm everywhere.

It's your attention that comes and goes,
half inside, half outside,
twirling, trailing, knotted and tied.

Sometimes I'm an idea you get,
sometimes a terror that comes upon you,
sometimes I make you sick

and sometimes I'm just there
a color that goes
with everything you wear,

an invisible crown
winging closer
settling in your hair, a strand

of song
floating like a veil,
calling you

to realize, to remember,
that wherever you are,
I am

wrapping you in righteousness,
jeweling you with fire,
wedding your affliction

to my compassion, your once
to my forever.
It's true.

I'm yours—
I've always been—
the moment you say *I do*.

# Acknowledgments

This book was supported by a research fellowship from Hadassah Brandeis Institute, long a nurturer of creative work about gender, Judaism, and Jewishness, which also gave me opportunities to read from and speak about the project.

These poems would never have become what they are without the encouragement, wisdom, and challenging and insightful comments of Nancy Mayer, who helped from beginning to end. I also want to thank Liz Denlinger and Annie Kantar for important interventions, and Dan Libenson of JewishLive.org, who facilitated the online "Containing Multitudes" conversations and community where preliminary versions of the book premiered.

Several of these poems have been published, in somewhat different versions, in *Poetry* ("Forgetting" and "Comfort Animal"); *Poetry International* ("Fragmentation"); *Ritualwell* ("Revelation"); *Moment* ("Singing"); and *Tikkun* ("Ready").

Joy Ladin has published nine previous books of poetry, including National Jewish Book Award winner *The Book of Anna*, reissued in a revised edition by EOAGH Press in 2021; a memoir of gender transition, National Jewish Book Award finalist *Through the Door of Life*; and Lambda Literary and Triangle Award finalist, *The Soul of the Stranger: Reading God and Torah from a Transgender Perspective*. Episodes of her online conversation series, "Containing Multitudes," are available at www.jewishlive.org/multitudes; links to her writings, readings, interviews and talks are at her website, joyladin.wordpress.com.

Other books from selva oscura press

*Durations* by Ted Pearson

*Why Letter Ellipsis* by Kimberly Alidio

*Alameda* by Broc Rossell

*Mood Indigo* by Jeanne Heuving

*Veronica: A Suite in X Parts* by Erica Hunt

*Eroding Witness* by Nathaniel Mackey

*afterKleist* by Matthew Fink

*A Spell in the Pokey: Selected Poems by Hugh Walthall* edited by Aldon Lynn Nielsen

*Zippers & Jeans* by J. Peter Moore

*Moment's Omen* by Nathaniel Mackey

*dog with elizabethan collar* by Ken Taylor


And by Three Count Pour
(an imprint of selva oscura press)

*Breath and Precarity* by Nathaniel Mackey

*No Hierarchy of the Lovely: Ten Uncollected Essays and Other Prose 1939–1981* by Robert Duncan
edited by James Maynard

*Songs In-Between the Day / Offshore St. Mark* by David Need
—Durham Suite: 5—

*Anuncio's Last Love Song* by Nathaniel Mackey

*Southern Colortype* by J. Peter Moore

*first the trees, now this* by Ken Taylor

*A History of Fire* by Dianne Timbin

*[Distressed Properties]* by Magdalena Zurawski

selvaoscurapress.com